SMOKER COOKBOOK

COMPLETE SMOKER COOKBOOK FOR SMOKING AND GRILLING, ULTIMATE BBQ BOOK WITH TASTY RECIPES FOR YOUR OUTDOOR SMOKER AND GRILL

BY ADAM JONES

TABLE OF CONTENTS

INTRODUCTION

Where there is a smoke, there is a flavor. Smoking meat or making BBQ is not only a means of cooking but for some individuals and classy enthusiasts, this is a form of Art! Or dare I say a form of lifestyle! Enthusiasts all around the world have been experimenting and dissecting the secrets of perfectly smoked meat for decades now, and in our golden age, perhaps they have cracked it up completely!In our age, the technique of Barbequing or Smoking meat has been perfected to such a level, that a BBQ Grill is pretty much an essential amenity found in all backyard or sea-beach parties!

This is the drinking fountain for the more hip and adventurous people, who prefer to have a nice chat with their friends and families while smoking up a few batches of Burger Patty for them to enjoy. But here's the thing, while this art might seem as a very easy form of cooking which only requires you to flip meats over and over! Mastering it might be a little bit difficult if you don't know have the proper information with you. This guide is an essential book for beginners who want to smoke meat without needing expert help from others. This book offers detailed guidance obtained by years of smoking meat, includes clear instructions and step-by-step directions for every recipe. This is the only guide you will ever need to professionally smoke a variety of food. The book includes full-color photographs of every finished meal to make your job easier. Whether you are a beginner meat smoker or looking to go beyond the basics, the book gives you the tools and tips you need to start that perfectly smoked meat. Smoking is something has withstood the test of time, it will continue to stand the test of time for years to come. Not only is it a method to preserve your catch or kill, but it's also one of if not the best-tasting food there is.

CHAPTER-1 BEEF

SPICY SWEET SMOKED BEEF ROAST BLACK PEPPER

(COOKING TIME 4 HOURS 10 MINUTES)

INGREDIENTS FOR 10 SERVINGS

- Beef roast (3.5-lb., 1.6-kg.)

The Rub

- Brown sugar – ½ cup
- Kosher salt – 2 tablespoons
- Black pepper – 1 tablespoon
- Smoked paprika – 1 ½ tablespoons
- Garlic powder – 1 tablespoon
- Onion powder – 1 tablespoon
- Ground mustard – ½ tablespoon
- Cayenne pepper – ½ tablespoon

The Heat

- Use charcoal and Alder wood chunks for indirect smokes.

The Water Pan

- Water – 1 cup
- Apple juice – 1 cup

Method

1. Prepare a grill and set it for indirect heat.
2. Place charcoal and starters in a grill then ignite the starters. Put the burning charcoal on one side of the grill.
3. Place a heavy-duty aluminum pan then place on the other side of the grill.
4. Fill the aluminum pan with water and apple juice then place wood chunks on the burning charcoal.

5. Set the grill grate then cover the grill with the lid and set the temperature to 225°F (107°C).

6. Next, rub the beef roast with brown sugar, kosher salt, black pepper, smoked paprika, garlic powder, onion powder, ground mustard, and cayenne pepper. Set aside.

7. Once the smoke is ready, place the seasoned brisket in the grill and smoke the brisket for 4 hours. Add more charcoal if needed and control the temperature using the vent.

8. Check the internal temperature of the smoked beef roast and once it reaches 125°F (52°C), remove the smoked beef roast from the grill and place on a serving dish.

9. Cut the smoked beef roast into slices then serve.

10. Enjoy!

Smoked Beef Prime Ribs Cocoa with Sugar Brown Glaze

(Cooking time 3 Hours 30 Minutes)

Ingredients for 10 servings

- Beef Prime Ribs (6-lb., 2.7-kg.)

The Rub

- Cocoa powder – 2 tablespoons

- Kosher salt – 2 tablespoons

- Black pepper – 1 ½ tablespoons

- Brown sugar – ½ cup

- Beef bouillon – 2 tablespoons

- Onion powder – 1 tablespoon

- Oregano – ½ teaspoon

- Thyme – ¾ teaspoon

- Cumin – ¾ teaspoon

- Cayenne pepper – 1 teaspoon

- Smoked paprika – 1 ½ teaspoons

THE GLAZE

- Butter – ½ cup

- Brown sugar – ½ cup

- Maple syrup – ¼ cup

- Apple cider vinegar – ½ cup

THE HEAT

- Use charcoal and Cherry wood chunks for indirect smokes.

THE WATER PAN

- Apple juice – 2 cups

METHOD

1. Combine the rub ingredients—cocoa powder, kosher salt, black pepper, brown sugar, beef bouillon, onion powder, oregano, thyme, cumin, cayenne pepper, and smoked paprika in a bowl then stir until the mixture is well mixed.

2. Rub the beef prime ribs with the spice mixture then let it rest for approximately an hour.

3. Next, prepare the grill and set it for indirect heat.

4. Place charcoal and starters in a grill then ignite the starters. Put the burning charcoal on one side of the grill.

5. Place a heavy-duty aluminum pan then place on the other side of the grill.

6. Fill the aluminum pan with apple juice then place wood chunks on the burning charcoal.

7. Set the grill grate then cover the grill with the lid and set the temperature to 225°F (107°C).

8. Once the grill is ready, place the seasoned beef prime ribs on the grate and smoke for 2 hours.

9. In the meantime, melt butter in a saucepan then add brown sugar, maple syrup, and apple cider vinegar. Stir until incorporated then set aside.

10. After 2 hours of smoking, open the lid and baste the beef prime ribs with the glaze mixture.

11. Flip the beef prime ribs and baste with the remaining glaze mixture.

12. Continue smoking the beef prime ribs for an hour and a half or until the internal temperature has reached 125°F (52°C) for medium doneness or 145°F (63°C for well-done.

13. Remove the smoked beef prime ribs from the grill and transfer to a serving dish.

14. Serve and enjoy warm.

Comfort Smoked Coffee Mocha Beef Tenderloin

(Cooking time 4 Hours 10 Minutes)

Ingredients for 10 servings

- Beef Tenderloin (5-lb., 2.3-kg.)

The Rub

- Ground coffee – ¼ cup

- Cocoa powder – ¼ cup

- Brown sugar – ½ cup

- Kosher salt – 1 tablespoon

- Paprika – 1 tablespoon
- Cinnamon – 1 ½ tablespoons
- Cayenne pepper – 1 teaspoon

THE GLAZE

- Butter – 2 tablespoons
- Maple syrup – 2 tablespoons

THE HEAT

- Use charcoal and Oak wood chunks for indirect smokes.

THE WATER PAN

- Water– 2 cups
- Espresso coffee – 3 tablespoons

METHOD

1. Prepare a grill and set for indirect heat.

2. Place charcoal and starters in a grill then ignite the starters. Put the burning charcoal on one side of the grill.

3. Place a heavy-duty aluminum pan then place on the other side of the grill.

4. Pour water into the aluminum pan then add espresso coffee into the water pan. Stir until incorporated.

5. Place wood chunks on the burning charcoal then close the grill with the lid.

6. Adjust the temperature to 225°F (107°C) and wait until the grill is ready.

7. Once the grill has reached the desired temperature, place the seasoned beef tenderloin on the grate and smoke for 4 hours.

8. Using the vent, control the temperature and regularly check the internal temperature of the beef tenderloin.

9. When the internal temperature of the smoked beef tenderloin has reached 120°F (49°C), remove from the grill and transfer to a serving dish.

10. Quickly baste the smoked beef tenderloin with butter then splash maple syrup over the smoked beef tenderloin.

11. Cut the smoked beef tenderloin into slices then serve.

12. Enjoy!

Rich Smoked Beef Tri-Tip with Tomato Ketchup and Whiskey Glaze

(Cooking time 4 Hours 10 Minutes)

Ingredients for 10 servings

- Beef Tri-Tip (4-lbs., 1.8-kg.)

The Rub

- Kosher salt – 2 tablespoons
- Black pepper – 1 tablespoon
- Onion powder – 1 tablespoon
- Garlic powder – ¾ tablespoon

- Cayenne powder – ½ teaspoon
- Thyme – ¾ tablespoon
- Rosemary – ½ tablespoon
- Coriander – ½ tablespoon

THE GLAZE

- Ketchup – ½ cup
- Tomato paste – ¼ cup
- Whiskey – 3 tablespoons
- Apple cider vinegar – 2 tablespoons
- Worcestershire sauce – 1 tablespoon
- Molasses – 2 tablespoons
- Black pepper – 1 teaspoon
- Cayenne pepper – ½ teaspoon

THE HEAT

- Use charcoal and Pecan wood chunks for indirect smokes.

THE WATER PAN

- Water– 2 cups

METHOD

1. Combine the rub ingredients—kosher salt, black pepper, onion powder, garlic powder, cayenne powder, thyme, rosemary, and coriander. Stir until the spices are mixed well.

2. Rub the beef tri-tip with the spice mixture then set aside.

3. Next, prepare a grill and set for indirect heat.

4. Place charcoal and starters in a grill then ignite the starters. Put the burning charcoal on one side of the grill.

5. Place a heavy-duty aluminum pan then place on the other side of the grill.

6. Fill the aluminum pan with water then set the temperature of the grill to 225°F (107°C).

7. Once the smoke is ready, place the seasoned beef tri-tip on the grate inside the grill and smoke for 4 hours.

8. In the meantime, place the glaze ingredients—ketchup, tomato paste, whiskey, apple cider vinegar, Worcestershire sauce, molasses, black pepper, and cayenne pepper in a bowl then stir until incorporated.

9. After 3 hours of smoking, baste the glaze mixture all over the beef tri-tip then continue smoking for another hour or until the internal temperature of the smoked beef tri-tip has reached 120°F (49°C).

10. Remove the smoked beef tri-tip from the grill and transfer to a serving dish.

11. Quickly score the smoked beef tri-tip at several places then baste the remaining glaze over the beef tri-tip.

12. Serve and enjoy!

Oregano Paprika Smoked Brisket Barbecue

(Cooking time 6 Hours 10 Minutes)

Ingredients for 10 servings

- Beef brisket (4-lbs., 1.8-kg.)

The Rub

- Paprika – ½ cup

- Oregano – 1 ¼ tablespoons

- Brown sugar – ½ cup

- Kosher salt – ¼ cup

- Ground mustard – 1 tablespoon

- Black pepper – ½ tablespoon

- Coriander – ½ tablespoon

- Garlic powder – 1 ¼ tablespoons

- Onion powder – 1 ¼ tablespoons

THE GLAZE

- Beef broth – ¾ cup

- Ketchup – 6 tablespoons

- Molasses – 3 tablespoons

- Diced onion – 1 cup

- Worcestershire sauce – 1 ½ tablespoons

- Brown mustard – ¾ tablespoon

- Cider vinegar – 1 ½ tablespoons

- Hot sauce – 1 ½ teaspoons

- Spice rub mixture – 2 tablespoons

- Liquid smoke – ¾ teaspoon

THE HEAT

- Use charcoal and Alder wood chunks for indirect smokes.

THE WATER PAN

- Water – 1 cup

- Beer – 1 cup

METHOD

1. Combine the rub ingredients—paprika, oregano, brown sugar, kosher salt, ground mustard, black pepper, coriander, garlic powder, and onion powder in a bowl then stir the spices until mixed.

2. Take two tablespoons of the rub mixture then place in a bowl. Set aside.

3. Rub the beef brisket with the remaining rub mixture then let it rest for approximately an hour.

4. Next, prepare the grill and set it for indirect heat.

5. Place charcoal and starters in a grill then ignite the starters. Put the burning charcoal on one side of the grill.

6. Place a heavy-duty aluminum pan then place on the other side of the grill.

7. Fill the aluminum pan with water and beer then place wood chunks on the burning charcoal.

8. Set the grill grate then cover the grill with the lid and set the temperature to 225°F (107°C).

9. Once the smoke is ready, place the seasoned brisket in the grill and smoke the brisket for 6 hours. Control the temperature using the vent and add more charcoal if it is necessary.

10. Meanwhile, pour beef broth into a saucepan then add ketchup, molasses, diced onion, Worcestershire sauce, brown mustard, cider vinegar, hot sauce, and liquid smoke.

11. Add the rub mixture to the saucepan then stir well. Bring to a simmer and remove from heat.

12. After 5 hours of smoking, open the lid and baste the brisket with the glaze mixture.

13. Continue smoking for an hour and once the internal temperature has reached 185°F (85°C), open the grill and take the smoked brisket out of the grill.

14. Place the smoked brisket on a serving dish then serve.

15. Enjoy!

Chapter-2 Pork

Honey Glazed Smoked Pork Butt with Chili Cayenne Rub

(Cooking time 6 Hours 10 Minutes)

Ingredients for 10 servings

- Pork Butt (4-lbs., 1.8-kg.)

The Rub

- Cumin – 1 tablespoon
- Paprika – 1 tablespoon

- Garlic powder – 1 ½ tablespoons

- Onion powder – 1 tablespoon

- Chili powder – ¾ tablespoon

- Brown sugar – 1 ½ tablespoons

- Kosher salt – 1 tablespoon

- Cayenne pepper – ¾ teaspoon

- Black pepper – ¾ teaspoon

THE GLAZE

- Brown sugar – ¾ cup

- Honey – 3 tablespoons

- Mustard – ¾ tablespoon

- Worcestershire sauce – 1 ½ teaspoons

- Cinnamon – 1 teaspoon

- Ginger – ½ teaspoon

THE HEAT

- Use charcoal and Alder wood chunks for indirect smokes.

THE WATER PAN

- Water – 2 cups

- Ginger – 1 teaspoon

METHOD

1. Score the pork butt at several places then rub with cumin, paprika, garlic powder, onion powder, chili powder, brown sugar, kosher salt, cayenne pepper, and black pepper.

2. Prepare the grill and set it for indirect heat.

3. Place charcoal and starters in a grill then ignite the starters. Put the burning charcoal on one side of the grill.

4. Place a heavy-duty aluminum pan then put it on the other side of the grill.

5. Pour water into the aluminum pan then add ginger to the pan. Stir until the ginger is completely dissolved.

6. Set the grill grate then cover the grill with the lid and set the temperature to 225°F (107°C).

7. Once the grill has reached the desired temperature, place the seasoned pork butt on the grate inside the grill and smoke for 4 hours. Control the temperature and add more charcoal if it is necessary.

8. Meanwhile, place the entire glaze ingredients in a bowl then stir until incorporated.

9. After 4 hours of smoking, baste the pork with half of the glaze mixture and continue smoking for 2 hours.

10. Check the internal temperature of the smoked pork butt and once it reaches 170°F (77°C), remove the smoked pork butt from the grill and transfer to a serving dish.

11. Quickly baste the smoked pork butt with the remaining glaze mixture then serve.

12. Enjoy!

Spicy Smoked Pork Rib with Special Coffee Rub

(Cooking time 5 Hours 10 Minutes)

Ingredients for 10 servings

- Pork Ribs (5-lb., 2.3-kg.)

THE RUB

- Dried chilies – 2 ½ tablespoons
- Dried chipotle peppers – 2 ½ tablespoons
- Ground coffee – 1 ¼ tablespoons
- Garlic powder – ½ tablespoon
- Onion powder – ½ tablespoon
- Kosher salt – ½ tablespoon
- Brown sugar – ½ tablespoon

THE GLAZE

- Soy sauce – ¾ cup
- Hot chili sauce – 2 tablespoons
- Brown sugar – ¼ cup
- Sesame oil – 1 ½ tablespoons
- Garlic powder – 1 teaspoon
- Ginger – ½ teaspoon
- Applesauce – 2 tablespoons

THE HEAT

- Use charcoal and Cherry wood chunks for indirect smokes.

THE WATER PAN

- Apple juice – 2 cups

METHOD

1. Combine the rub ingredients—dried chilies, dried chipotle peppers, ground coffee, garlic powder, onion powder, kosher salt, and brown sugar in a bowl then mix until the spices are well mixed.

2. Remove the excess fats from the pork ribs then rub with the spice mixture. Let it rest for an hour.

3. Next, prepare the grill and set it for indirect heat.

4. Place charcoal and starters in a grill then ignite the starters. Put the burning charcoal on one side of the grill.

5. Place a heavy-duty aluminum pan then put it on the other side of the grill.

6. Pour apple juice into the aluminum pan and put the grill grate on top.

7. Set the temperature to 225°F (107°C) and wait until it reaches the desired temperature.

8. Once the smoke is ready, place the seasoned pork ribs on the grate inside the grill then smoke for 4 hours. Control the temperature and add more charcoal if it is necessary.

9. In the meantime, place the glaze mixture—soy sauce, hot chili sauce, brown sugar, sesame oil, garlic powder, ginger, and applesauce in a bowl then stir until incorporated.

10. After 4 hours of smoking, baste the pork ribs with half of the glaze mixture and continue smoking for another hour or until the internal temperature has reached 160°F (71°C).

11. Remove the smoked pork ribs from the grill the quickly baste the remaining glaze over the smoked pork ribs.

12. Serve and enjoy!

Sweet Smoked Pork Tenderloin with Apple Wedges

(Cooking time 6 Hours 10 Minutes)

Ingredients for 10 servings

- Pork Tenderloin (4-lbs., 1.8-kg.)
- Fresh Ripe Apples -2

THE RUB

- Brown sugar – 2 tablespoons
- Cumin – 1 teaspoon
- Garlic powder – 1 tablespoon
- Onion powder – 1 tablespoon
- Kosher salt – ½ tablespoon
- Black pepper – ½ teaspoon

THE GLAZE

- Butter – 3 tablespoon
- Balsamic vinegar – 3 tablespoons
- Honey – 3 tablespoons
- Garlic powder – 1 teaspoon
- Dried oregano – ½ teaspoon
- Dried basils – ½ teaspoon
- Dries thyme – ½ teaspoon
- Black pepper – ¼ teaspoon

THE HEAT

- Use charcoal and Peach wood chunks for indirect smokes.

THE WATER PAN

- Apple juice – 2 cups

METHOD

1. Prepare the grill and set for indirect heat.

2. Place charcoal and starters in a grill then ignite the starters. Put the burning charcoal on one side of the grill.

3. Place a heavy-duty aluminum pan then put it on the other side of the grill.

4. Pour apple juice into the aluminum pan and put the grill grate on top.

5. Set the temperature to 225°F (107°C) and wait until it reaches the desired temperature.

6. Cut and make several neat slits on the pork tenderloin. Make sure that you do not cut the pork tenderloin through the bottom side.

7. Rub the pork tenderloin with the rub ingredients—brown sugar, cumin, garlic powder, onion powder, kosher salt, and black pepper.

8. Next, core the apples and cut into thin wedges.

9. Put a slice of apple at every slit and once the smoke is ready, place the pork tenderloin on the grate inside the grill.

10. Smoke the pork tenderloin for 5 hours and using the vent, control the temperature. Add more charcoal and wood chunks if it is necessary.

11. In the meantime, melt butter in a saucepan over low heat then let it cool for a few minutes.

12. Add balsamic vinegar, honey, garlic powder, oregano, basil, thyme, and black pepper then stir until incorporated.

13. After 6 hours of smoking or once the internal temperature has reached 160°F (71°C), remove the smoked pork loin from the grill.

14. Quickly baste the smoked pork tenderloin with the glaze mixture then serve.

15. Enjoy!

Nourishing Smoke Pork Chops with Orange Marmalade

(Cooking time 5 Hours 10 Minutes)

Ingredients for 10 servings

- Pork Chops (4-lbs., 1.8-kg.)

The Rub

- Kosher salt – 2 tablespoons

- Cumin – 1 ½ tablespoons

- Pepper – 1 tablespoon

- Coriander – ¾ tablespoon

- Garlic powder – 2 teaspoons

- Cayenne pepper – 2 teaspoons

The Glaze

- Orange juice – 1 cup
- Orange marmalade – ¾ cup
- Orange zest – ½ teaspoon
- Sugar – ½ cup
- Cinnamon – 1 teaspoon
- Ground cloves- ¼ teaspoon

The Heat

- Use charcoal and Pear wood chunks for indirect smokes.

The Water Pan

- Water – 1 cup
- Orange juice – 1 cup
- Kaffir lime leaves – 3

METHOD

1. Combine the rub ingredients—kosher salt, cumin, pepper, coriander, garlic powder, cayenne pepper in a bowl then stir until incorporated.

2. Rub the pork chops with the spice mixture then let it rest for at least 2 hours. Store the seasoned pork chops in a container with a lid and keep in the fridge to keep it fresh.

3. Next, pour orange juice in a bowl then add orange marmalade, orange zest, sugar, cinnamon, and ground clove. Stir the mixture until incorporated.

4. After that, take the seasoned pork out of the fridge and thaw at room temperature.

5. Prepare the grill and set for indirect heat.

6. Place charcoal and starters in a grill then ignite the starters. Put the burning charcoal on one side of the grill.

7. Place a heavy-duty aluminum pan then put it on the other side of the grill.

8. Pour water and orange juice into the aluminum pan then put kaffir lime leaves in it.

9. Set the grill grate on top then set the temperature to 225°F (107°C) and wait until it reaches the desired temperature.

10. Once the grill is ready, place the seasoned pork chops on the grate inside the grill then baste with the glaze mixture.

11. Cover the grill with the lid and smoke the pork chops for 5 hours. Maintain the temperature and add more charcoal if it is necessary.

12. Once the internal temperature of the smoked pork chops has reached 160°F (71°C), remove from the grill and quickly baste with the remaining glaze mixture.

13. Serve and enjoy.

Caramelized and Juicy Smoked Pulled Pork with Healthy Sage

(Cooking time 8 Hours 10 Minutes)

Ingredients for 10 servings

- Pork Shoulders (6-lb., 2.7-kg.)

THE INJECTION

- Apple juice – 2 cups
- Pineapple juice – 2 cups
- Worcestershire sauce – 2 ½ tablespoons
- Soy sauce – 1 ½ tablespoons
- Salt – 1 tablespoon
- Brown sugar -1 ½ tablespoons

THE GLAZE

- Butter – ¼ cup
- Brown sugar – ¼ cup
- Sage – 2 tablespoons
- Black pepper – 1 teaspoon
- Onion powder – ½ teaspoon

THE HEAT

- Use charcoal and Pear wood chunks for indirect smokes.

THE WATER PAN

- Water – 2 cups

METHOD

1. Pour apple juice and pineapple juice into a container then add Worcestershire sauce, soy sauce, salt, and brown sugar. Stir the liquid until incorporated.

2. Fill an injector with the liquid mixture then inject the pork shoulder at several places.

3. Next, melt butter over low heat then mix with brown sugar, sage, black pepper, and onion powder. Stir until well mixed then set aside.

4. Prepare the grill and set for indirect heat.

5. Place charcoal and starters in a grill then ignite the starters. Put the burning charcoal on one side of the grill.

6. Place a heavy-duty aluminum pan then put it on the other side of the grill.

7. Pour water and orange juice into the aluminum pan then put kaffir lime leaves in it.

8. Set the grill grate on top then set the temperature to 225°F (107°C) and wait until it reaches the desired temperature.

9. Once the grill is ready, place the seasoned pork shoulders on the grate inside the grill then baste with the glaze mixture.

10. Smoke the pork shoulder for 8 hours and quickly baste with the remaining glaze mixture once every 2 hours.

11. Check and maintain the temperature of the grill then add more charcoal and wood chunks if it is needed.

12. Once it is done and the internal temperature of the smoked pork has reached 205°F (96°C), remove the smoked pork from the grill and place on a flat surface.

13. Using a fork or a sharp knife shred the smoked pork and place on a serving dish.

14. Serve and enjoy!

Chapter-3 Lamb

Tropical Smoked Lamb Ribs Pineapple Rum

(Cooking time 5 Hours 10 Minutes)

Ingredients for 10 servings

- Lamb Ribs (6-lb., 2.7-kg.)

THE RUB

- Brown sugar – ¾ cup
- Kosher salt – 1 ½ tablespoons
- Coriander – 2 tablespoons
- Black pepper – ¾ tablespoon
- Garlic powder – 1 ½ tablespoons
- Onion powder – 1 ½ tablespoons
- Thyme – ½ tablespoon
- Allspice – ¾ tablespoon
- Cinnamon – 1 tablespoon
- Chili powder – ¾ tablespoon

THE SPRAY

- Pineapple juice – 1 cup

THE GLAZE

- Pineapple juice – 1 cup
- Apple cider vinegar – 1 tablespoon
- Butter – ¼ cup
- Black pepper – 1 teaspoon
- Onion powder – 1 tablespoon
- Garlic powder – 1 tablespoon
- Jamaican Rum – ¼ cup

THE SAUCE

- Pineapple juice – 2 cups

- Hot sauce – 2 tablespoons

- Chopped cilantro – 2 tablespoons

- Ginger – ½ teaspoon

- Ketchup – ½ cup

- Cider vinegar – 2 tablespoons

- Worcestershire sauce – 1 ½ tablespoons

- Brown sugar – ¼ cup

- Soy sauce – 1 tablespoon

- Black pepper – ½ teaspoon

THE HEAT

- Use charcoal and Cherry wood chunks for indirect smokes.

THE WATER PAN

- Apple juice – 2 cups

METHOD

1. Remove the excess fat from the lamb ribs then rub with brown sugar, coriander, kosher salt, black pepper, garlic powder, onion powder, thyme, allspice, cinnamon, and chili powder.

2. Prepare the grill and set it for indirect heat.

3. Place charcoal and starters in a grill then ignite the starters. Put the burning charcoal on one side of the grill.

4. Place a heavy-duty aluminum pan then put it on the other side of the grill.

5. Pour apple juice into the aluminum pan then set the grate on the grill.

6. Adjust the temperature to 225°F (107°C) and wait until it reaches the desired temperature.

7. In the meantime, melt butter over low heat then mix with pineapple juice and apple cider vinegar.

8. Season the glaze mixture with black pepper, onion powder, and garlic powder then stir until incorporated.

9. Add Jamaican rum to the glaze mixture then stir well.

10. Once the grill is ready, place the seasoned lamb ribs on the grate then baste with the glaze mixture.

11. Smoke the seasoned lamb ribs for 5 hours and spray with pineapple juice once every hour.

12. Meanwhile, place the entire sauce ingredients—pineapple juice, hot sauce, chopped cilantro, ginger, ketchup, cider vinegar, Worcestershire sauce, brown sugar, soy sauce, and black pepper in a bowl then stir the sauce mixture until incorporated. Set aside.

13. Once the internal temperature of the smoked lamb ribs has reached 135°F (57°C), remove from the grill and place on a serving dish.

14. Drizzle the sauce over the smoked lamb ribs and then serve with the remaining sauce.

Smoked Lamb Shoulder Rosemary Garlic

(Cooking time 6 Hours 10 Minutes)

Ingredients for 10 servings

- Lamb Shoulder (6-lb., 2.7-kg.)

The Rub

- Garlic powder – ½ tablespoon

- Chopped fresh rosemary – 3 tablespoons

- Onion powder – ½ tablespoon

- Cider vinegar – 2 tablespoons

- Brown sugar – 3 tablespoons

- Kosher salt – 3 tablespoons
- Oregano – ½ tablespoon

THE HEAT

- Use charcoal and Oak wood chunks for indirect smokes.

THE WATER PAN

- Beer – 2 cups

METHOD

1. Prepare the grill and set it for indirect heat.

2. Place charcoal and starters in a grill then ignite the starters. Put the burning charcoal on one side of the grill.

3. Place a heavy-duty aluminum pan then put it on the other side of the grill.

4. Pour beer into the aluminum pan then set the grate on the grill.

5. Adjust the temperature to 225°F (107°C) and wait until it reaches the desired temperature.

6. Score the lamb shoulder at several places then rub with garlic powder, onion powder, cider vinegar, brown sugar, kosher salt, and oregano.

7. Rub chopped fresh rosemary over the lamb shoulder then fill it to the cuts.

8. When the grill is ready, place the seasoned lamb shoulder on the grate inside the grill and smoke for 6 hours.

9. Check the heat and control the temperature. Add more charcoal and wood chunks if it is necessary.

10. Once the smoked lamb shoulder is tender or the internal temperature has reached 135°F (57°C), remove from the grill and place on a serving dish.

11. Serve and enjoy!

SMOKED LAMB MINT WITH CRUNCHY PISTACHIO RUB

(COOKING TIME 7 HOURS 10 MINUTES)

INGREDIENTS FOR 10 SERVINGS

- Rack of Lamb (7-lb., 3.2-kg.)

THE RUB

- Minced garlic – 2 tablespoons

- Chopped mint leaves – ¼ cup

- Olive oil – ¼ cup

- Kosher salt – 2 ½ tablespoons

- Cumin – ½ tablespoon

- Fennel – ¼ tablespoon

- Coriander – 1 teaspoon

- Roasted pistachio – 1 cup

- Brown sugar – 2 tablespoons

THE GLAZE

- Molasses – 3 tablespoons

THE HEAT

- Use charcoal and Oak wood chunks for indirect smokes.

THE WATER PAN

- Water – 2 cups

METHOD

1. Place minced garlic, mint leaves, kosher salt, cumin, fennel, coriander, roasted pistachio, and brown sugar in a blender then drizzle olive oil over the spices. Blend until smooth and set aside.

2. Prepare the grill and set it for indirect heat.

3. Place charcoal and starters in a grill then ignite the starters. Put the burning charcoal on one side of the grill.

4. Place a heavy-duty aluminum pan then put it on the other side of the grill.

5. Pour water into the aluminum pan then set the grate on the grill.

6. Adjust the temperature to 225°F (107°C) and wait until it reaches the desired temperature.

7. Score the lamb at several places then cover the lamb with the mint and pistachios mixture. Make sure that the lamb is completely coated with the spice mixture.

8. When the grill has reached the desired temperature, place the coated lamb on the grate and smoke for 7 hours.

9. Maintain the heat and control the temperature. Add more charcoal and wood chunks if it is needed.

10. Once the internal temperature has reached 135°F (57°C), remove the smoked lamb from the grill. The smoked lamb will be tender.

11. Transfer the smoked lamb to a serving dish then baste molasses over the smoked lamb.

12. Serve and enjoy!

Cinnamon Honey Tea Smoked Lamb Leg

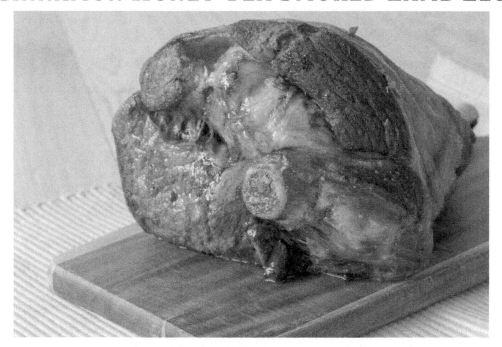

(Cooking time 5 Hours 10 Minutes)

Ingredients for 10 servings

- Lamb Legs (5-lb., 2.3-kg.)

The Rub

- Ground Oolong Tea – 3 tablespoons
- Espresso beans – ¾ tablespoon
- Ground peppercorns – ¾ tablespoon
- Onion powder – ½ tablespoon
- Garlic powder – ½ tablespoon
- Kosher salt – ½ tablespoon

THE GLAZE

- Honey - ¼ cup

- Brown sugar – ¼ cup

- Dried tea leaves – 2 teaspoons

- Hot water – ¼ cup

- Lemon juice – 2 tablespoons

- Allspice – ¼ teaspoon

- Cinnamon – ½ teaspoon

- Cayenne pepper – ½ teaspoon

THE HEAT

- Use charcoal and Cherry wood chunks for indirect smokes.

THE WATER PAN

- Water – 2 cups

METHOD

1. Prepare the grill and set it for indirect heat.

2. Place charcoal and starters in a grill then ignite the starters. Put the burning charcoal on one side of the grill.

3. Place a heavy-duty aluminum pan then put it on the other side of the grill.

4. Pour water into the aluminum pan then set the grate on the grill.

5. Adjust the temperature to 225°F (107°C) and wait until it reaches the desired temperature.

6. While waiting for the grill, place the rub ingredients—ground oolong tea, espresso beans, ground peppercorns, onion powder, garlic powder, and kosher salt in a food processor then process the spices until smooth and well combined.

7. Score the lamb leg at several places then rub the spice mixture over the lamb leg.

8. When the grill is ready, place the seasoned lamb leg on the grate inside the grill and smoke for 5 hours. Maintain the heat and control the temperature.

9. In the meantime, add dried-tea leaves to the hot water and let it rest for about 2 minutes.

10. Strain the tea water and discard the dried-tea leaves.

11. Pour honey into the tea water then add brown sugar, lemon juice, allspice, cinnamon, and cayenne pepper. Stir the glaze mixture until incorporated.

12. At the last hour of smoking, baste the lamb leg with half of the glaze mixture then continue smoking for another hour.

13. Once the smoked lamb leg is done or the internal temperature of the smoked lamb leg has reached 135°F (57°C), remove it from the grill and transfer to a serving dish.

14. Quickly baste the smoked lamb leg with the remaining glaze mixture then serve.

15. Enjoy!

STICKY SWEET APRICOT ON SMOKED LAMB RIBS

(COOKING TIME 6 HOURS 10 MINUTES)

INGREDIENTS FOR 10 SERVINGS

- Lamb Ribs (5-lb., 2.3-kg.)

THE RUB

- Brown sugar – ¼ cup

- Kosher salt – 2 tablespoons

- Dried oregano – 1 ½ tablespoons

- Dried basil – 1 tablespoon

THE GLAZE

- Apricot preserves – 1 cup
- Ketchup – ¼ cup
- Brown sugar – 2 ½ tablespoons
- Olive oil – 1 ½ tablespoons
- Soy sauce – 1 tablespoon
- Ginger – ½ teaspoon

THE HEAT

- Use charcoal and Apple wood chunks for indirect smokes.

THE WATER PAN

- Apple juice – 2 cups

METHOD

1. Prepare the grill and set it for indirect heat.
2. Place charcoal and starters in a grill then ignite the starters. Put the burning charcoal on one side of the grill.
3. Place a heavy-duty aluminum pan then put it on the other side of the grill.
4. Pour water into the aluminum pan then set the grate on the grill.
5. Adjust the temperature to 225°F (107°C) and wait until it reaches the desired temperature.
6. Rub the lamb ribs with brown sugar; kosher salt, dried oregano, and dried basil then let it rest for a few minutes.

7. Next, place the seasoned lamb ribs on the grate inside the grill and smoke the lamb ribs for 6 hours. Using the vent, control the temperature and add more charcoal or wood chunks if it is necessary.

8. In the meantime, combine apricot preserves with ketchup, brown sugar, olive oil, soy sauce, and ginger then stir until incorporated.

9. At the last hour of smoking, baste the lamb ribs with the apricot glaze once every 15 minutes.

10. Once the internal temperature of the smoked lamb ribs has reached 135°F (57°C) or the smoked lamb has become tender enough, remove it from the grill

11. Place the smoked lamb ribs on a serving dish and serve.

12. Enjoy warm!

Chapter-4 POULTRY

Hot Smoked Chicken Wings Chili Paprika

(Cooking time 2 Hours 10 Minutes)

Ingredients for 10 servings

- Chicken wings (5-lb., 2.3-kg.)

THE RUB

- Olive oil – 1 ½ tablespoon

- Chili powder - 2 tablespoons

- Smoked paprika – 2 tablespoons

- Cumin – ¾ teaspoon

- Onion powder – 1 ½ teaspoons

- Garlic powder – 1 ½ teaspoons

- Kosher salt   - 1 ½ teaspoons

- Ground pepper – 2 teaspoons

- Cayenne – 1 ½ teaspoons

THE HEAT

- Use charcoal and Apple wood chunks for indirect smokes.

THE WATER PAN

- Apple juice – 2 cups

METHOD

1. Prepare the grill and set it for indirect heat.

2. Place charcoal and starters in a grill then ignite the starters. Put the burning charcoal on one side of the grill.

3. Place a heavy-duty aluminum pan then place on the other side of the grill.

4. Pour apple juice into the aluminum pan and place wood chunks on top of the burning charcoal then set the grill grate.

5. Cover the grill with the lid and set the temperature to 275°F (135°C).

6. In the meantime, combine olive oil with chili powder, smoked paprika, cumin, onion powder, garlic powder, kosher salt, ground pepper, and cayenne. Mix until incorporated.

7. Rub the chicken wings with the spice mixture and once the grill is ready, place the chicken wings on the grate above the water pan.

8. Smoke the chicken for approximately 2 hours and using the vent control the temperature.

9. Check the burning charcoal and add more charcoal and wood chunks if it is necessary.

10. After 2 hours of smoking, check the internal temperature of the smoked chicken and once it reaches 170°F (77°C), remove the smoked chicken wings from the grill. It is done enough.

11. Arrange the chicken wings on a serving dish then serve warm.

12. Enjoy!

BALSAMIC HONEY SMOKED CHICKEN THIGHS

(COOKING TIME 3 HOURS 10 MINUTES)

Ingredients for 10 servings

- Chicken Thighs (3-lb., 1.4-kg.)

The Rub

- Kosher salt – 1 tablespoon
- Onion powder – 1 tablespoon
- Pepper – 2 tablespoons
- Garlic powder – ¾ tablespoon
- Paprika – 2 tablespoons

The Glaze

- Balsamic vinegar – ½ cup
- Honey – ¼ cup
- Mustard – 1 tablespoon
- Minced garlic – 2 tablespoons
- Black pepper – ½ teaspoon

The Heat

- Use charcoal and Alder wood chunks for indirect smokes.

The Water Pan

- Apple juice – 2 cups

METHOD

1. Score the chicken thighs at several places then rub with kosher salt, onion powder, pepper, garlic powder, and paprika.

2. Place the seasoned chicken thighs in a container with a lid and marinate for 2 hours. Store in the fridge to keep them fresh.

3. Next, combine balsamic vinegar with honey and mustard then season the glaze mixture with minced garlic and pepper. Stir the glaze mixture until incorporated.

4. After 2 hours in the fridge, take the seasoned chicken thighs and dip in the glaze mixture. Let them rest for at least 15 minutes.

5. Next, prepare the grill and set it for indirect heat.

6. Place charcoal and starters in a grill then ignite the starters. Put the burning charcoal on one side of the grill.

7. Place a heavy-duty aluminum pan then place on the other side of the grill.

8. Pour apple juice into the aluminum pan and place wood chunks on top of the burning charcoal then set the grill grate.

9. Cover the grill with the lid and set the temperature to 275°F (135°C).

10. When the grill is ready, place the glazed chicken thighs on the grate inside the grill and smoke for 3 hours.

11. Once the internal temperature of the smoked chicken thighs has reached 170°F (77°C), baste the remaining glaze mixture over the smoked chicken thighs and smoke for another 10 minutes.

12. Remove the smoked chicken thighs from the grill and transfer to a serving dish.

13. Serve and enjoy!

Smoked Turkey Lemon Soda Chili

(Cooking time 6 Hours 10 Minutes)

Ingredients for 10 servings

- Whole Turkey (3-lb., 1.4-kg.)

The Rub

- Olive oil – 3 tablespoons
- Garlic powder – 2 tablespoons
- Onion powder – 1 tablespoon
- Chili powder – ¾ tablespoon
- Paprika – 1 teaspoon
- Kosher salt – 1 tablespoon

THE FILLING

- Fresh rosemary – 1 cup
- Fresh basil – 1 cup
- Garlic cloves – 5
- Sliced lemon – ½ cup

THE GLAZE

- Soda – 1 cup
- Brown sugar – ¼ cup
- Soy sauce – 2 tablespoons
- White vinegar – 1 tablespoon
- Lemon juice – 2 tablespoons
- Garlic powder – 1 teaspoon
- Paprika – ½ teaspoon
- Cayenne pepper – ½ teaspoon
- Black pepper – ½ teaspoon

THE HEAT

- Use charcoal and Oak wood chunks for indirect smokes.

THE WATER PAN

- Water – 2 cups

- Lemon juice – 2 tablespoons

- Ginger – 1 teaspoon

- Lemon grass - 1

- Bay leaves - 2

METHOD

1. Add garlic powder, onion powder, chili powder, paprika, and kosher salt to olive oil then stir until mixed.

2. Rub the turkey with the spice mixture then fill the turkey cavity with fresh rosemary, fresh basils, garlic cloves, and sliced lemon. Let it rest for an hour.

3. Next, prepare the grill and set it for indirect heat.

4. Place charcoal and starters in a grill then ignite the starters. Put the burning charcoal on one side of the grill.

5. Place a heavy-duty aluminum pan then place on the other side of the grill.

6. Pour water into the aluminum pan then add lemon juice, ginger, lemon grass, and bay leaves to the water stir until just combined.

7. Place wood chunks on top of the burning charcoal then set the grill grate.

8. Cover the grill with the lid and set the temperature to 275°F (135°C).

9. When the grill is ready, place the seasoned turkey on the grate inside the smoker and smoke for 3 hours. Control the temperature and add more charcoal or wood chunks if it is necessary.

10. In the meantime, pour soda into a heavy duty aluminum pan then season with soy sauce, brown sugar, white vinegar, lemon juice, garlic powder, paprika, cayenne pepper, and black pepper. Stir until incorporated.

11. After 3 hours of smoking, take the turkey out of the grill and transfer to the aluminum pan with glaze mixture.

12. Baste the glaze mixture over the turkey and return back the turkey in the aluminum pan to the grill.

13. Smoke the turkey for another 3 hours and once the internal temperature of the smoked turkey has reached 170°F (77°C), remove it from the grill.

14. Place the smoked turkey on a serving dish and cut into slices.

15. Serve and enjoy.

MAPLE SMOKED CHICKEN DRUMSTICKS WITH TOMATO BARBECUE SAUCE

(COOKING TIME 2 HOURS 10 MINUTES)

INGREDIENTS FOR 10 SERVINGS

- Chicken Drumsticks (4-lbs., 1.8-kg.)

THE RUB

- Kosher salt – 1 tablespoon

- Pepper – ½ teaspoon

- Maple syrup – ½ cup

- Brown sugar – 3 tablespoons

65

The Sauce

- Butter – 2 tablespoons
- Tomato sauce – 1 cup
- Cider vinegar – 2 tablespoons
- Rice vinegar – 1 ½ tablespoons
- Molasses – 3 tablespoons
- Worcestershire sauce – 2 tablespoons
- Brown sugar – 1 tablespoon
- Mustard – ¾ tablespoon
- Hot sauce – 1 teaspoon
- Salt – ¼ teaspoon
- Black pepper – 1 teaspoon
- Cayenne pepper – ¼ teaspoon

The Heat

- Use charcoal and Maple wood chunks for indirect smokes.

The Water Pan

- Water – 2 cups
- Brown sugar – 2 tablespoons

METHOD

1. Place maple syrup and brown sugar in a bowl then stir well. Set aside.

2. Rub the chicken drumsticks with salt and pepper then let it rest for a few minutes.

3. Next, prepare the grill and set it for indirect heat.

4. Place charcoal and starters in a grill then ignite the starters. Put the burning charcoal on one side of the grill.

5. Place a heavy-duty aluminum pan then place on the other side of the grill.

6. Pour water into the aluminum pan then add brown sugar to the pan. Stir until the brown sugar is completely dissolved.

7. Place wood chunks on top of the burning charcoal then set the grill grate.

8. Cover the grill with the lid and set the temperature to 275°F (135°C).

9. When the grill is ready, arrange the seasoned chicken drumsticks on the grate inside the grill and baste with the maple syrup mixture.

10. Smoke the chicken drum sticks for 2 hours and baste the remaining maple syrup mixture over the chicken drum sticks once every 30 minutes.

11. In the meantime, melt butter over low heat and let it cool for a few minutes.

12. Add tomato sauce, cider vinegar, rice vinegar, molasses, brown sugar, Worcestershire sauce, mustard, hot sauce, salt, black pepper, and cayenne pepper then stir until the sauce is incorporated.

13. When the internal temperature of the smoked chicken drumsticks has reached 170°F (77°C), remove from the grill and arrange on a serving dish.

14. Drizzle the tomato barbecue sauce on top and serve.

15. Enjoy warm.

Smoked Sweet Chicken Teriyaki with Aromatic Sesame

(Cooking time 2 Hours 10 Minutes)

Ingredients for 10 servings

- Chicken Wings (3-lb., 1.4-kg.)

THE RUB

- Brown sugar – ¼ cup
- Paprika – ½ tablespoon
- Ginger – 1 teaspoon
- Kosher salt – ½ teaspoon
- Sesame oil – 3 tablespoons

THE SAUCE

- Soy sauce – ½ cup
- Cooking sherry – ¼ cup
- Sesame oil – 3 tablespoons
- Brown sugar – ¼ cup
- Ginger – 1 teaspoon
- Pineapple juice – ½ cup

THE TOPPING

- Sesame seeds – ¼ cup

THE HEAT

- Use charcoal and Peach wood chunks for indirect smokes.

THE WATER PAN

- Water – 2 cups

METHOD

1. Rub the chicken wings with brown sugar, paprika, ginger, and salt then let them rest for an hour. Store in the fridge to keep the chicken wings fresh.

2. Next, prepare the grill and set it for indirect heat.

3. Place charcoal and starters in a grill then ignite the starters. Put the burning charcoal on one side of the grill.

4. Place a heavy-duty aluminum pan then place on the other side of the grill.

5. Pour water into the aluminum pan and place wood chunks on top of the burning charcoal. Set the grill grate on top.

6. Cover the grill with the lid and set the temperature to 275°F (135°C).

7. When the grill is ready, arrange the seasoned chicken wings on the grate inside the grill and smoke for an hour.

8. In the meantime, place the entire sauce ingredients—soy sauce, cooking sherry, sesame oil, ginger, brown sugar, and pineapple juice in a heavy-duty aluminum pan. Stir until the sauce is incorporated.

9. After an hour of smoking, take the smoked chicken wings out of the grill and transfer to the sauce mixture. Stir a bit until the chicken wings are completely coated with the sauce.

10. Return the chicken wings in the aluminum pan with sauce to the grill and smoke the chicken wings for another hour.

11. Once it is done and the internal temperature of the smoked chicken wings has reached 170°F (77°C), remove them from the grill and arrange on a serving dish.

12. Sprinkle sesame seeds on top and serve.

13. Enjoy!

CHAPTER-5 FISH

BUTTERY BOURBON SMOKED SALMON FILLET

(COOKING TIME 3 HOURS 10 MINUTES)

INGREDIENTS FOR 10 SERVINGS

- Salmon fillet (3-lb., 1.4-kg.)

THE MARINADE

- Kosher salt – ½ tablespoon
- Black pepper – 1 teaspoon
- Orange marmalade – 1 cup
- Bourbon – ½ cup
- Brown sugar – 3 tablespoons
- Cayenne pepper – ½ teaspoon
- Butter – 2 tablespoons

THE GLAZE

- Butter – 3 tablespoons
- Brown sugar – 1 tablespoon

THE HEAT

- Use charcoal and Alder wood chunks for indirect smokes.

THE WATER PAN

- Water – 2 cups
- Ginger – ½ teaspoon

METHOD

1. Melt butter over low heat then mix with kosher salt, black pepper, orange marmalade, bourbon, brown sugar, and cayenne pepper.

2. Rub the salmon fillet with the spice mixture and marinate for 30 minutes.

3. Next, prepare the grill and set it for indirect heat.

4. Place charcoal and starters in a grill then ignite the starters. Put the burning charcoal on one side of the grill.

5. Place a heavy-duty aluminum pan then place on the other side of the grill.

6. Pour water into the aluminum pan and add ginger to the water. Stir until the ginger is dissolved.

7. Place wood chunks on top of the burning charcoal then set the grill grate.

8. Cover the grill with the lid and set the temperature to 200°F (93°C).

9. Place the seasoned salmon on the grate inside the grill and smoke the salmon for 3 hours.

10. Once the smoked salmon is tender, open the lid and quickly baste butter over the salmon.

11. Sprinkle brown sugar on top and baste again with the remaining butter.

12. Transfer the smoked salmon to a serving dish then serve.

13. Enjoy!

SMOKED TROUT TENDER WITH MIXED HERBS

(COOKING TIME 3 HOURS 10 MINUTES)

INGREDIENTS FOR 10 SERVINGS

- Trout Fillet (3-lb., 1.4-kg.)

THE RUB

- Olive oil – 3 tablespoons
- Dried rosemary – 1 ½ teaspoons
- Dried thyme – 1 teaspoon
- Diced parsley – 1 tablespoon
- Garlic powder – 2 teaspoons
- Cayenne pepper – ½ teaspoon
- Black pepper – 1 teaspoon
- Kosher salt – ¾ tablespoon

THE HEAT

- Use charcoal and Oak wood chunks for indirect smokes.

THE WATER PAN

- Water – 2 cups
- Ginger – ½ teaspoon
- Turmeric – ½ teaspoon
- Lemon grass - 1

METHOD

1. Combine dried rosemary with thyme, parsley, garlic powder, cayenne pepper, black pepper, and kosher salt then stir until well mixed.

2. Baste the trout fillet with olive oil then sprinkle the spice mixture over the trout fillet.

3. Next, prepare the grill and set it for indirect heat.

4. Place charcoal and starters in a grill then ignite the starters. Put the burning charcoal on one side of the grill.

5. Place a heavy-duty aluminum pan then place on the other side of the grill.

6. Pour water into the aluminum pan then stir in ginger, turmeric, and lemon grass.

7. Place wood chunks on top of the burning charcoal then set the grill grate.

8. Cover the grill with the lid and set the temperature to 200°F (93°C).

9. Arrange the trout on the grate inside the grill and smoke for 3 hours. The smoked trout will be tender.

10. Once it is done, remove the smoked trout from the grill and place on a serving dish.

11. Serve and enjoy.

TROPICAL SIMPLE SMOKED ALBACORE FILLET

(COOKING TIME 3 HOURS 10 MINUTES)

INGREDIENTS FOR 10 SERVINGS

- Albacore fillet (3-lb., 1.4-kg.)

THE RUB

- Kosher salt – 1 tablespoon

- Brown sugar – ½ cup

- Lemon juice – 3 tablespoons

- Grated lemon zest – ½ teaspoon

- Grated orange zest – ½ teaspoon

The Heat

- Use charcoal and Cherry wood chunks for indirect smokes.

The Water Pan

- Orange juice – 2 cups

- Cinnamon – ½ teaspoon

Method

1. Splash lemon juice over the albacore fillet then rub with kosher salt, brown sugar, grated lemon zest, and grated orange zest.

2. Marinate the albacore fillet for 2 hours and store in the fridge to keep it fresh.

3. Next, prepare the grill and set it for indirect heat.

4. Place charcoal and starters in a grill then ignite the starters. Put the burning charcoal on one side of the grill.

5. Place a heavy-duty aluminum pan then place on the other side of the grill.

6. Pour orange juice into the aluminum pan then add cinnamon to the water pan. Stir until incorporated.

7. Place wood chunks on top of the burning charcoal then set the grill grate.

8. Cover the grill with the lid and set the temperature to 200°F (93°C).

9. Wait until the grill is ready then place the seasoned albacore fillet on the grate inside the grill.

10. Smoke the seasoned albacore for 2 to 3 hours or until the smoked albacore is flaky.

11. Once it is done, remove from the grill and transfer the smoked albacore fillet to a serving dish.

12. Serve and enjoy

GINGERY HOISIN SMOKED TILAPIA WITH BUTTER GLAZE

(COOKING TIME 3 HOURS 10 MINUTES)

INGREDIENTS FOR 10 SERVINGS

- Tilapia Fillet (3-lb., 1.4-kg.)

THE MARINADE

- Brown sugar – 1 ½ cups
- Soy sauce – ¾ cup
- Hoisin sauce – 3 tablespoons
- Ginger – 1 teaspoon
- Cayenne pepper – ½ teaspoon
- Garlic powder – 1 teaspoon
- Lemon juice – 2 tablespoons

THE GLAZE

- Butter – 3 tablespoons
- Hoisin sauce – ½ cup
- Sriracha sauce – 1 tablespoon

THE HEAT

- Use charcoal and Alder wood chunks for indirect smokes.

THE WATER PAN

- Orange juice – 2 cups

METHOD

1. Combine the marinade ingredients—brown sugar, soy sauce, hoisin sauce, ginger, cayenne pepper, garlic powder, and lemon juice in a zipper-lock plastic bag. Stir until mixed.

2. Add tilapia fillet to the plastic bag and shake until the tilapia is completely coated with the spice mixture.

3. Marinate the tilapia for 2 hours and store in the fridge to keep it fresh.

4. Next, prepare the grill and set it for indirect heat.

5. Place charcoal and starters in a grill then ignite the starters. Put the burning charcoal on one side of the grill.

6. Place a heavy-duty aluminum pan then place on the other side of the grill.

7. Pour orange juice into the aluminum pan then place wood chunks on top of the burning charcoal.

8. Set the grate inside the grill and adjust the temperature to 200°F (93°C).

9. When the grill is ready, take the seasoned tilapia and place on the grate inside the grill. Smoke the tilapia for 3 hours.

10. In the meantime, melt butter over very low heat then stir in Hoisin sauce and Sriracha sauce.

11. Once the smoked tilapia is done, open the grill and baste the smoked tilapia with the glaze mixture.

12. Cover the grill with the lid and wait for 5 minutes.

13. Remove the smoked tilapia from the grill and transfer to a serving dish.

14. Drizzle the remaining glaze mixture over the smoked tilapia then serve.

15. Enjoy!

CHAPTER-6 SEAFOOD

NOURISHING LEMON BUTTER SMOKED CRAB LEGS

(COOKING TIME 20 MINUTES)

INGREDIENTS FOR 10 SERVINGS

- Crab Legs (5-lb., 2.3-kg.)

THE GLAZE

- Butter – 1 ½ cups

- Lemon juice – ¼ cup

- Diced parsley – 1 tablespoon

- Grated lemon zest – ½ teaspoon

- Salt – ¼ teaspoon

THE HEAT

- Use charcoal and Alder wood chunks for indirect smokes.

THE WATER PAN

- Water – 2 cups

- Lemongrass – 1

METHOD

1. Prepare the grill and set it for indirect heat.

2. Place charcoal and starters in a grill then ignite the starters. Put the burning charcoal on one side of the grill.

3. Place a heavy-duty aluminum pan then place on the other side of the grill.

4. Pour water into the aluminum pan and add lemongrass to the water.

5. Place wood chunks on top of the burning charcoal then set the grill grate.

6. Cover the grill with the lid and set the temperature to 200°F (93°C).

7. While waiting for the grill, melt butter over medium heat then stir in lemon juice, grated lemon zest, diced parsley, and salt to the melted butter. Mix until incorporated.

8. Once the grill is ready, baste the glaze mixture over the crab legs and arrange on the grate inside the grill.

9. Smoke the crab legs for 20 minutes and once it is done, remove from the grill.

10. Transfer the smoked crab legs to a serving dish then baste with the remaining glaze mixture.

11. Serve and enjoy!

Sweet Lemon Pepper Smoked Lobster Tails

(Cooking time 35 Minutes)

Ingredients for 10 servings

- Lobster (6-lb., 2.7-kg.)

THE GLAZE

- Butter – ¼ cup

- Kosher salt – 2 tablespoons

- Brown sugar – 2 ½ tablespoons

- Black pepper – 1 teaspoon

- Grated lemon zest – ½ teaspoon

- Onion powder – 1 teaspoon

- Garlic powder – 1 teaspoon

THE HEAT

- Use charcoal and Alder wood chunks for indirect smokes.

THE WATER PAN

- Water – 2 cups

- Lemon juice – 1 tablespoon

METHOD

1. Melt butter over medium heat then add brown sugar and salt to the melted butter. Stir until dissolved.

2. Next, season the melted butter with black pepper, grated lemon zest, onion powder,

3. Prepare the grill and set it for indirect heat.

4. Place charcoal and starters in a grill then ignite the starters. Put the burning charcoal on one side of the grill.

5. Place a heavy-duty aluminum pan then place on the other side of the grill.

6. Pour water into the aluminum pan and add lemon juice to the water.

7. Place wood chunks on top of the burning charcoal then set the grill grate.

8. Cover the grill with the lid and set the temperature to 200°F (93°C).

9. Baste the butter mixture over the lobster legs then arrange on the grate inside the smoker.

10. Smoke the lobster legs for 35 minutes or until flake.

11. Remove the smoked lobster legs from the grill and transfer to a serving dish.

12. Baste the remaining butter mixture over the smoked lobsters and serve.

13. Enjoy!

Citrus Smoked Scallops with Alder Aroma

(Cooking time 3 Hours 5 Minutes)

Ingredients for 10 servings

- Scallops (3-lb., 1.4-kg.)

The Rub

- Kosher salt – 1 tablespoon
- Pepper – 1 teaspoon

THE SAUCE

- Butter – ¼ cup

- Garlic powder – 1 teaspoon

- Grated orange zest – ½ teaspoon

- Orange juice – 1 cup

- Worcestershire sauce – ½ teaspoon

- Diced parsley – 1 tablespoon

- Pepper – ½ teaspoon

THE HEAT

- Use charcoal and Alder wood chunks for indirect smokes.

THE WATER PAN

- Orange juice – 2 cups

METHOD

1. Rub the scallops with salt and pepper then set aside.

2. Prepare the grill and set it for indirect heat.

3. Place charcoal and starters in a grill then ignite the starters. Put the burning charcoal on one side of the grill.

4. Place a heavy-duty aluminum pan then place on the other side of the grill.

5. Pour orange juice into the water pan then place wood chunks on top of the burning charcoal. Set the grill grate.

6. Cover the grill with the lid and set the temperature to 200°F (93°C).

7. While waiting for the grill, melt butter over medium heat then mix with orange juice.

8. Season the mixture with grated orange zest, garlic powder, Worcestershire sauce, diced parsley, and pepper then stir until incorporated.

9. Arrange the scallops in a heavy-duty aluminum pan then pour the butter mixture over the scallops.

10. When the grill is ready, place the aluminum pan in the grill then smoke the scallops for 3 hours.

11. Once it is done, remove the smoked scallops from the grill and transfer to a serving dish.

12. Serve and enjoy!

Juicy Smoked Oyster with Walnut Oil

(Cooking time 3 Hours 5 Minutes)

Ingredients for 10 servings

- Oyster without shells (3-lb., 1.4-kg.)

The Marinade

- Kosher salt – 2 tablespoon

- White wine – 1 cup

- Walnut oil – ¼ cup

- Beer – 1 cup

THE HEAT

- Use charcoal and Apple wood chunks for indirect smokes.

THE WATER PAN

- Beer – 2 cups

METHOD

1. Pour beer and walnut oil in a container then add salt and white wine. Stir the mixture until incorporated.

2. Add the oysters to the container and marinate for at least 2 hours. Store in the fridge to keep them fresh.

3. Prepare the grill and set it for indirect heat.

4. Place charcoal and starters in a grill then ignite the starters. Put the burning charcoal on one side of the grill.

5. Place a heavy-duty aluminum pan then place on the other side of the grill.

6. Pour beer into the water pan then place wood chunks on top of the burning charcoal. Set the grill grate.

7. Cover the grill with the lid and set the temperature to 200°F (93°C).

8. Take the oysters out of the marinade and transfer to a heavy-duty aluminum pan.

9. Place the aluminum pan in the grill and smoke the oyster for 3 hours or until tender.

10. Once it is done, remove from the grill and transfer the smoked oysters to a serving dish.

11. Serve and enjoy.

CHAPTER-7 GAME

SPICED SMOKED VENISON TENDER

(COOKING TIME 7 HOURS 10 MINUTES)

INGREDIENTS FOR 10 SERVINGS

- Venison (5-lb., 2.3-kg.)

THE RUB

- Black pepper – 3 tablespoons
- Paprika – 2 tablespoons
- Kosher salt – 1 ½ tablespoons
- Garlic powder – 1 tablespoon
- Onion powder – 1 tablespoon
- Cayenne pepper – ¾ tablespoon
- Coriander – ¾ tablespoon
- Dill – ½ tablespoon

THE HEAT

- Use charcoal and Alder wood chunks for indirect smokes.

THE WATER PAN

- Beef broth – 2 cups
- Ginger – ½ teaspoon
- Lemon grass - 1

METHOD

1. Rub the venison with black pepper, paprika, kosher salt, garlic powder, onion powder, cayenne pepper, coriander, and dill.

2. Prepare the grill and set it for indirect heat.

3. Place charcoal and starters in a grill then ignite the starters. Put the burning charcoal on one side of the grill.

4. Place a heavy-duty aluminum pan then place on the other side of the grill.

5. Pour beef broth into the aluminum pan then add ginger and lemongrass to the broth.

6. Place wood chunks on top of the burning charcoal then set the grill grate.

7. Cover the grill with the lid and set the temperature to 200°F (93°C).

8. Wait until the grill reaches the desired temperature then place the seasoned venison on the grate inside the grill.

9. Maintain the heat and control the temperature. Add more charcoal and wood chunks if it is necessary.

10. Once the internal temperature of the smoked venison has reached 160°F (71°C), remove from the grill and transfer to a serving dish.

11. Serve and enjoy.

Cinnamon Smoked Quails Orange Tea

(Cooking time 1 Hour 10 Minutes)

Ingredients for 10 servings

- Quails (6-lb., 2.7-kg.)

THE RUB

- Sichuan peppercorns – ¼ cup
- Kosher salt – 2 tablespoons
- Grated orange zest – 1 teaspoon
- Ginger – 1 teaspoon
- Tea leaves – 1 cup
- Brown sugar – 1 cup
- Cinnamon – 1 teaspoon
- Cloves – 2
- Olive oil – ¼ cup
- Lemon juice – 3 tablespoons

THE HEAT

- Use charcoal and Apple wood chunks for indirect smokes.

THE WATER PAN

- Orange juice – 2 cups

METHOD

1. Combine Sichuan peppercorns with kosher salt, grated orange zest, ginger, tea leaves, brown sugar, cinnamon, and cloves

2. Pour olive oil and lemon juice over the spice mixture then stir until incorporated.

3. Rub the quails with the spice mixture and marinate for at least 3 hours. Store in the fridge to keep the quails fresh.

4. Prepare the grill and set it for indirect heat.

5. Place charcoal and starters in a grill then ignite the starters. Put the burning charcoal on one side of the grill.

6. Place a heavy-duty aluminum pan then place on the other side of the grill.

7. Pour orange juice into the aluminum pan then place wood chunks on top of the burning charcoal. Set the grill grate.

8. Cover the grill with the lid and set the temperature to 200°F (93°C).

9. Place the seasoned quails on the grate inside the grill then smoke for 2 hours.

10. Once the smoked quails are done, or the internal temperature of the smoked quails has reached 160°F (71°C), remove from the grill and transfer to a serving dish.

11. Serve and enjoy.

SPICY AND HOT SMOKED RABBIT BARBECUE

(COOKING TIME 3 HOURS 10 MINUTES)

INGREDIENTS FOR 10 SERVINGS

- Rabbit (6-lb., 2.7-kg.)

THE BRINE

- Kosher salt – 2 tablespoons

- White vinegar – ½ cup

- Water – 1 quart

THE RUB

- Garlic powder – 2 tablespoons
- Cayenne pepper – 1 tablespoon
- Kosher salt – 1 tablespoon
- Black pepper – 1 tablespoon

THE GLAZE

- Garlic powder – 2 tablespoons
- Diced jalapeno pepper – 2 teaspoons
- Cayenne pepper – 1 teaspoon
- Olive oil – 2 tablespoons
- Ketchup – 2 cups
- Brown sugar – 1 cup
- Apple cider vinegar – 1 cup
- Apple juice – ½ cup
- Honey – ½ cup
- Worcestershire sauce – 1 tablespoon
- Kosher salt – 1 teaspoon
- Black pepper – 1 teaspoon

THE HEAT

- Use charcoal and Hickory wood chunks for indirect smokes.

The Water Pan

- Apple juice – 2 cups

Method

1. Pour water into a container then stir in kosher salt and white vinegar.

2. Score the rabbit at several places then put the rabbit into the brine. Soak the rabbit for at least an hour.

3. After an hour, take the rabbit out of the brine then wash and rinse it. pat the rabbit dry.

4. Prepare the grill and set it for indirect heat.

5. Place charcoal and starters in a grill then ignite the starters. Put the burning charcoal on one side of the grill.

6. Place a heavy-duty aluminum pan then place on the other side of the grill.

7. Pour apple juice into the aluminum pan then place wood chunks on top of the burning charcoal. Set the grill grate.

8. Cover the grill with the lid and set the temperature to 200°F (93°C).

9. Combine the rub ingredients—garlic powder, cayenne pepper, kosher salt, and black pepper in a bowl then mix well.

10. Rub the rabbit with the spice mixture then place on the grate inside the grill. Smoke the seasoned rabbit for 3 hours.

11. Maintain the heat and control the temperature. Add more charcoal and wood chunks if it is needed.

12. Next, pour olive oil, ketchup, apple juice, apple cider vinegar, and honey into a bowl then season with garlic powder, diced jalapeno pepper, cayenne pepper, brown sugar, Worcestershire sauce, salt, and pepper then stir until incorporated.

13. After 15 minutes of smoking, baste the rabbit with the glaze mixture and repeat once every 30 minutes.

14. Once the smoked rabbit is tender and the internal temperature of the smoked rabbit has reached 170°F (77°C), remove it from the grill.

15. Place the smoked rabbit on a serving dish and serve.

16. Enjoy!

Chapter-8 VEGETABLES

Smoked Cheese Crumbles Stuffed Tomato

(Cooking time 1 Hour 30 Minutes)

Ingredients for 10 servings

- Large Red Tomatoes (3-lb., 1.4-kg.)

THE FILLING

- Butter – ¼ cup

- Minced garlic – 2 teaspoons

- Diced mushrooms – 1 cup

- Diced onion – ¼ cup

- Heavy cream – ¼ cup

- Diced bacon – ½ cup

- Grated Parmesan cheese – ¼ cup

- Grated cheddar cheese – ¼ cup

- Breadcrumbs – ¼ cup

THE TOPPING

- Grated Mozzarella cheese – ¼ cup

THE HEAT

- Use charcoal and Maple wood chunks for indirect smokes.

THE WATER PAN

- Water – 2 cups

- Cinnamon – 1 teaspoon

METHOD

1. Melt butter in a saucepan over low heat then stir in minced garlic, diced onion, and chopped mushroom. Sauté until wilted and aromatic then remove from the heat.

2. Add diced bacon, heavy cream, grated Parmesan cheese, grated cheddar cheese, and breadcrumbs to the melted butter then stir until combined.

3. Next, prepare the grill and set it for indirect heat.

4. Place charcoal and starters in a grill then ignite the starters. Put the burning charcoal on one side of the grill.

5. Place a heavy-duty aluminum pan then place on the other side of the grill.

6. Pour water into the aluminum pan then add cinnamon to the water.

7. Place wood chunks on top of the burning charcoal then set the grill grate.

8. Cover the grill with the lid and set the temperature to 225°F (107°C).

9. Cut the top of the tomatoes then scoop out the seeds.

10. Fill each tomato with the filling mixture then sprinkle grated Mozzarella cheese on top.

11. Arrange the tomatoes in a heavy-duty aluminum pan then place in the grill.

12. Smoke the stuffed tomatoes for an hour and a half or until wilted and warmed.

13. Once it is done, remove the smoked tomatoes from the grill and arrange on a serving dish.

14. Serve and enjoy.

Sweet Brown Chili Smoked Butternut Squash

(Cooking time 1 Hour 30 Minutes)

INGREDIENTS FOR 10 SERVINGS

- Whole Butternut Squash (2-lb., 0.9-kg.)

THE SPICES

- Olive oil – 3 tablespoons
- Kosher salt – 1 teaspoon
- Black pepper – 1 teaspoon
- Garlic powder – ½ teaspoon
- Brown sugar – 1 ½ tablespoons
- Chili powder – ¾ tablespoon

THE HEAT

- Use charcoal and Maple wood chunks for indirect smokes.

THE WATER PAN

- Water – 2 cups
- Cinnamon – 1 teaspoon

METHOD

1. Prepare the grill and set it for indirect heat.

2. Place charcoal and starters in a grill then ignite the starters. Put the burning charcoal on one side of the grill.

3. Place a heavy-duty aluminum pan then place on the other side of the grill.

4. Pour water into the aluminum pan then add cinnamon to the water.

5. Place wood chunks on top of the burning charcoal then set the grill grate.

6. Cover the grill with the lid and set the temperature to 225°F (107°C).

7. Add kosher salt, black pepper, garlic powder, brown sugar, and chili powder to olive oil then stir well.

8. Cut the butternut squash into halves lengthwise then discard the seeds.

9. Baste the olive oil and spice mixture over the halved butternut squash then place in the grill.

10. Smoke the butternut squash for approximately an hour and a half or until tender.

11. Once it is done, take the smoked butternut squash out of the grill and place on a serving dish.

12. Serve and enjoy.

Paprika Sage Smoked Mushrooms

(Cooking time 45 Minutes)

Ingredients for 10 servings

- Mushroom (2-lb., 0.9-kg.)

The Spices

- Kosher salt – ½ tablespoon

- Sage – ½ tablespoon

- Smoked paprika – ½ tablespoon

- Brown sugar – 2 tablespoons

THE HEAT

- Use charcoal and Maple wood chunks for indirect smokes.

THE WATER PAN

- Chicken broth – 2 cups

METHOD

1. Rub the mushrooms with salt, sage, smoked paprika, and brown sugar then spread over a heavy-duty aluminum pan.

2. Prepare the grill and set it for indirect heat.

3. Place charcoal and starters in a grill then ignite the starters. Put the burning charcoal on one side of the grill.

4. Place a heavy-duty aluminum pan then place on the other side of the grill.

5. Pour chicken broth into the aluminum pan then place wood chunks on top of the burning charcoal. Set the grill grate.

6. Cover the grill with the lid and set the temperature to 250°F (121°C).

7. Smoke the mushrooms for approximately 45 minutes or until tender and cooked through.

8. Once it is done, remove the smoked mushrooms from the grill and transfer to a serving dish.

9. Serve and enjoy.

SMOKED CABBAGE BUTTER BARBECUE

(COOKING TIME 1 HOUR 30 MINUTES)

INGREDIENTS FOR 10 SERVINGS

- Whole Cabbage (2-lb., 0.9-kg.)

THE SPICES

- Kosher salt – ½ teaspoon

- Pepper – ½ teaspoon

THE SAUCE

- Ketchup – ½ cup

- Apple cider vinegar – 2 tablespoons

- Lemon juice – 1 tablespoon

- Brown sugar – 2 tablespoons

- Worcestershire sauce – 1 tablespoon

- Mustard – ½ teaspoon

- Pepper – ½ teaspoon

- Smoked paprika – ½ teaspoon

- Onion powder – 1 teaspoon

- Garlic powder – 1 teaspoon

- Chili powder – 1 teaspoon

- Vegetable broth – ¼ cup

THE TOPPING

- Butter cubes – ¼ cup

THE HEAT

- Use charcoal and Maple wood chunks for indirect smokes.

THE WATER PAN

- Vegetable broth – 2 cups

METHOD

1. Prepare the grill and set it for indirect heat.

2. Place charcoal and starters in a grill then ignite the starters. Put the burning charcoal on one side of the grill.

3. Place a heavy-duty aluminum pan then place on the other side of the grill.

4. Pour chicken broth into the aluminum pan then place wood chunks on top of the burning charcoal. Set the grill grate.

5. Cover the grill with the lid and set the temperature to 200°F (93°C).

6. Cut the top of the cabbage then sprinkle salt and pepper over it. Set aside.

7. Combine the sauce ingredients—ketchup, apple cider vinegar, lemon juice, brown sugar, Worcestershire sauce, mustard, pepper, smoked paprika, onion powder, garlic powder, chili powder, and vegetable broth in a bowl then stir well.

8. Place cabbage in a heavy-duty aluminum pan then pour sauce over the cabbage. Make sure that the sauce flows into the slits between the cabbage leaves.

9. Top the cabbage with butter cubes then smoke for an hour and a half or until the smoked cabbage is tender and lightly golden brown.

10. Once it is done, remove the smoked cabbage from the grill and place on a serving dish.

11. Serve and enjoy.

CHAPTER-9 INFORMATION ON SMOKING MEAT

WHAT IS THE PRIMARY DIFFERENCE BETWEEN BARBEQUING A MEAT AND SMOKING IT?

You might not believe it, but there are still people who think that the process of Barbequing and Smoking are the same! So, this is something which you should know about before diving in deeper.

So, whenever you are going to use a traditional BBQ grill, you always put your meat directly on top of the heat source for a brief amount of time which eventually cooks up the meal. Smoking, on the other hand, will require you to combine the heat from your grill as well as the smoke to infuse a delicious smoky texture and flavor to your meat. Smoking usually takes much longer than traditional barbecuing. In most cases, it takes a minimum of 2 hours and a temperature of 100 -120 degrees for the smoke to be properly infused into the meat. Keep in mind that the time and temperature will obviously depend on the type of meat that you are using, and that is why it is suggested that you keep a meat thermometer handy to ensure that your meat is doing fine. Keep in mind that this method of barbecuing is also known as "Low and slow" smoking as well. With that cleared up, you should be aware that there are actually two different ways through which smoking is done.

THE CORE DIFFERENCE BETWEEN COLD AND HOT SMOKING

Depending on the type of grill that you are using, you might be able to get the option to go for a Hot Smoking Method or a Cold Smoking One. The primary fact about these three different cooking techniques which you should keep in mind are as follows:

- **Hot Smoking:** In this technique, the food will use both the heat on your grill and the smoke to prepare your food. This method is most suitable for items such as chicken, lamb, brisket etc.
- **Cold Smoking:** In this method, you are going to smoke your meat at a very low temperature such as 30 degree Celsius, making sure that it doesn't come into the direct contact with the heat. This is mostly used as a means to preserve meat and extend their life on the shelf.
- **Roasting Smoke:** This is also known as Smoke Baking. This process is essentially a combined form of both roasting and baking and can be performed in any type of smoker with a capacity of reaching temperatures above 82 degree Celsius.

By now you must be really curious to know about the different types of Smokers that are out there right?

Well, in the next section I am exactly going to discuss that!

THE DIFFERENT TYPES OF AVAILABLE SMOKERS

Essentially, what you should know is that right now in the market, you are going to get three different types of Smokers.

Charcoal Smoker

These types of smokers are hands down the best one for infusing the perfect Smoky flavor to your meat. But be warned, though, that these smokers are a little bit difficult to master as the method of regulating temperature is a little bit difficult when compared to normal Gas or Electric smokers.

Electric Smoker

After the charcoal smoker, next comes perhaps the simpler option, Electric Smokers. These are easy to use and plug and play type. All you need to do is just plug in, set the temperature and go about your daily life. The smoker will do the rest. However, keep in mind that the finishing smoky flavor won't be as intense as the Charcoal one.

Gas Smokers

Finally, comes the Gas Smokers. These have a fairly easy mechanism for temperature control and are powered usually by LP Gas. The drawback of these Smokers is that you are going to have to keep checking up on your Smoker every now and then to ensure that it has not run out of Gas.

Now, these have been further dissected into different styles of the smoker. Each of which is preferred by Smokers of different experiences.

THE DIFFERENT STYLES OF SMOKERS

The different styles of Smokers are essentially divided into the following.

Vertical (Bullet Style Using Charcoal)
These are usually low-cost solutions and are perfect for first-time smokers.

Vertical (Cabinet Style)
These Smokers come with a square shaped design with cabinets and drawers/trays for easy accessibility. These cookers also come with a water tray and a designated wood chips box as well.

Offset
These type of smokers have dedicated fireboxes that are attached to the side of the main grill. The smoke and heat required for these are generated from the firebox itself which is then passed through the main chamber and out through a nicely placed chimney.

Kamado Joe
And finally, we have the Kamado Joe which is ceramic smokers are largely regarded as being the "Jack Of All Trades".

These smokers can be used as low and slow smokers, grills, hi or low-temperature ovens and so on.

They have a very thick ceramic wall which allows it to hold heat better than any other type of smoker out there, requiring only a little amount of charcoal. These are easy to use with better insulation and are more efficient when it comes to fuel control.

With the smokers now set up, the next step is to understand about the woods used in the smoker. Below is a table which discusses most of the general types of woods that are used in Smokers and their potential benefits.

THE DIFFERENT TYPES OF WOOD AND THEIR BENEFITS

The Different Types Of Wood	Suitable For
Hickory	Wild game, chicken, pork, cheeses, beef
Pecan	Chicken, pork, lamb, cheeses, fish.
Mesquite	Beef and vegetables
Alder	Swordfish, Salmon, Sturgeon and other types of fishes. Works well with pork and chicken too.
Oak	Beef or briskets
Maple	Vegetable, ham or poultry
Cherry	Game birds, poultry or pork
Apple	Game birds, poultry, beef
Peach	Game birds, poultry or pork
Grape Vines	Beef, chicken or turkey
Wine Barrel Chips	Turkey, beef, chicken or cheeses
Seaweed	Lobster, mussels, crab, shrimp etc.
Herbs or Spices such as rosemary, bay leaves, mint, lemon peels, whole nutmeg etc.	Good for cheeses or vegetables and a small collection of light meats such as fillets or fish steaks.

THE BASIC PREPARATIONS

- Always be prepared to spend the whole day and take as much time as possible to smoke your meat for maximum effect.
- Make sure to obtain the perfect Ribs/Meat for the meal which you are trying to smoke. Do a little bit of research if you need.
- I have already added a list of woods in this book, consult to that list and choose the perfect wood for your meal.
- Make sure to prepare the marinade for each of the meals properly. A great deal of the flavor comes from the rubbing.
- Keep a meat thermometer handy to get the internal temperature when needed.
- Use mittens or tongs to keep yourself safe
- Refrain yourself from using charcoal infused alongside starter fluid as it might bring a very unpleasant odor to your food
- Always make sure to start off with a small amount of wood and keep adding them as you cook.
- Don't be afraid to experiment with different types of wood for newer flavor and experiences.
- Always keep a notebook near you and note jot down whatever you are doing or learning and use them during the future session. This will help you to evolve and move forward.

THE CORE ELEMENTS OF SMOKING!

Smoking is a very indirect method of cooking that relies on a number of different factors to give you the most perfectly cooked meal that you are looking for. Each of these components is very important to the whole process as they all work together to create the meal of your dreams.

- **Time**: Unlike grilling or even Barbequing, smoking takes a really long time and requires a whole lot of patience. It takes time for the smoky flavor to slowly get infused into the meats. Jus to bring things into comparison, it takes an about 8 minutes to fully cook a steak through direct heating, while smoking (indirect heating) will take around 35-40 minutes.

- **Temperature:** When it comes to smoking, the temperature is affected by a lot of different factors that are not only limited to the wind, cold air temperatures but also the cooking wood's dryness. Some smokers work best with large fires that are controlled by the draw of a chimney and restricted airflow through the various vents of the cooking chamber and firebox. While other smokers tend to require smaller fire with fewer coals as well as a completely different combination of the vent and draw controls. However, most smokers are designed to work at temperatures as low as 180 degrees Fahrenheit to as high as 300 degrees Fahrenheit. But the recommend temperature usually falls between 250 degrees Fahrenheit and 275 degrees Fahrenheit.

- **Airflow:** The level of air to which the fire is exposed to greatly determines how your fire will burn and how quickly it will burn the fuel. For instance, if you restrict air flow into the firebox by closing up the available vents, then the fire will burn at a low temperature and vice versa. Typically in smokers, after lighting up the fire, the vents are opened to allow for maximum air flow and is then adjusted throughout the cooking process to make sure that optimum flame is achieved.

- **Insulation:** Insulation is also very important when it comes to smokers as it helps to easily manage the cooking process throughout the whole cooking session. A good insulation allows smokers to efficiently reach the desired temperature instead of waiting for hours upon hours!

CONCLUSION

I can't express how honored I am to think that you found my book interesting and informative enough to read it all through to the end. I thank you again for purchasing this book and I hope that you had as much fun reading it as I had writing it. I bid you farewell and encourage you to move forward and find your true Smoked Meat spirit!

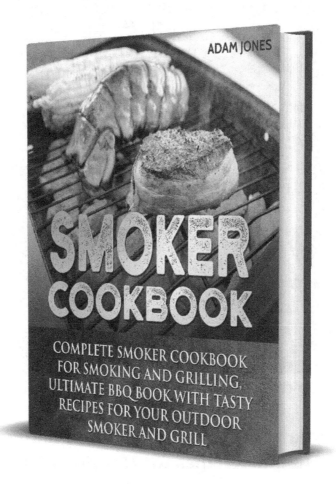

GET YOUR FREE GIFT

Subscribe to our Mail List and get your FREE copy of the book
'Smoking Meat: The Best 20 Recipes of Smoked Meat, Unique Recipes for Unique BBQ'

https://tiny.cc/smoke20

OTHER BOOKS BY ADAM JONES

https://www.amazon.com/dp/1731198760

https://www.amazon.com/dp/1070936340

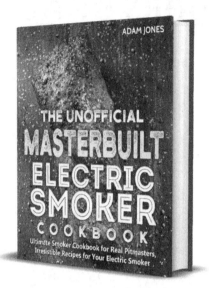

https://www.amazon.com/dp/1098708040

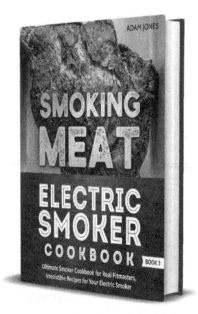

https://www.amazon.com/dp/1790483328

https://www.amazon.com/dp/1720321590

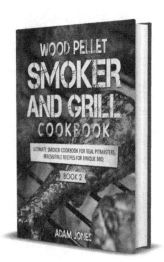

https://www.amazon.com/dp/1725577690

https://www.amazon.com/dp/1726837947

https://www.amazon.com/dp/1723009849

https://www.amazon.com/dp/B07DJ8XZT9

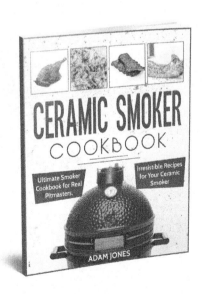

https://www.amazon.com/dp/B07DJ62MZP

https://www.amazon.com/dp/198756605X

https://www.amazon.com/dp/1548040959

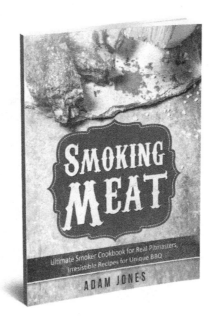

https://www.amazon.com/dp/B07B3R82P4

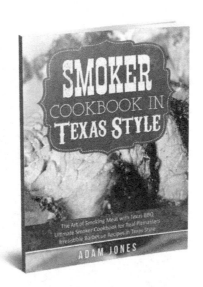

https://www.amazon.com/dp/B07B4YDKJ5

https://www.amazon.com/dp/1979559902

https://www.amazon.com/dp/1544791178

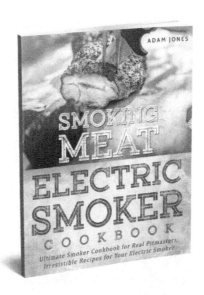

https://www.amazon.com/dp/1979811318

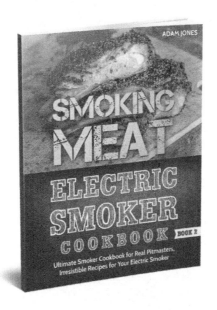

https://www.amazon.com/dp/1981617973

https://www.amazon.com/dp/1546605916

https://www.amazon.com/dp/1981940693

P.S. Thank you for reading this book. If you've enjoyed this book, please don't shy, drop me a line, leave a review or both on Amazon. I love reading reviews and your opinion is extremely important for me.

My Amazon page: www.amazon.com/author/adjones

Disclaimer and Terms of Use:*The effort has been made to ensure that the information in this book is accurate and complete, however, the author and the publisher do not warrant the accuracy of the information, text, and graphics contained within the book due to the rapidly changing nature of science, research, known and unknown facts and the internet. The Author and the publisher do not hold any responsibility for errors, omissions or contrary interpretation of the subject matter herein. This book is presented solely for motivational and informational purposes only.*

Made in the USA
Middletown, DE
11 May 2020